POOP

SUTRA

RED LIGHT, GREEN LIGHT

Sometimes you have to stay
still to do it!

If you happen to find yourself
standing at that moment, well
you have no choice...

but at least try to hit the hole!

HOLD ON TO TRADITIONS

In this case the push is so strong that you have to hold on to avoid suffering the backlash that could make you crash into the wall in front of you.

Be careful not to uproot the toilet paper holder!

EVEN THE NOBLES THEY DO THINGS

Well yes, even the most noble shit...

soft, hard, always smelly they make it!

The cacarella also affects the REs.

Devil's advocate

Have you ever gotten bored of routine?

So why not change everything, even how you poop!

Try the contrarian move, great for those who love change.

SOMEONE GOES TO THE BATHROOM, AND WHO GOES THERE IN STYLE

Going to shit is for everyone, but doing it in style is only for a few...

it's certainly not very comfortable, but some people just can't give up elegance!

CRIME ON THE TABLE OF THE CESS

The toilet is not free from crime scenes, of course one hopes at least that when it happens the victim has finished shitting...

always be careful to close the door and put the lock on the open window!

DJ SIT

Sometimes music can relax and help you do better, but also cover the harmful noises of a powerful shit... especially if you are at someone's house without certain confidences.

Classical music to taste good shit and powerful music to give a good push!

IT'S TOO MUCH FOR ME TOO

Usually the smell of other people's poop is terrible, not so much ours...

yet there are exceptions, in which case equip yourself with a gas mask, if you have one with military technology all the better!

You will need...

MAKE IT ROLL INSIDE

This is a touch of art but it's not for everyone... Stand upside down, legs in the air and aim at the toilet... then push as hard as you can and see where it will go!

MAKE ME MORE
ANOTHER ONE

Another touch of art, even greater difficulty...

here you will have to defeat the force of gravity and shoot a torpedo straight ahead!

Take a deep breath first, please, and be careful not to burst a vein!

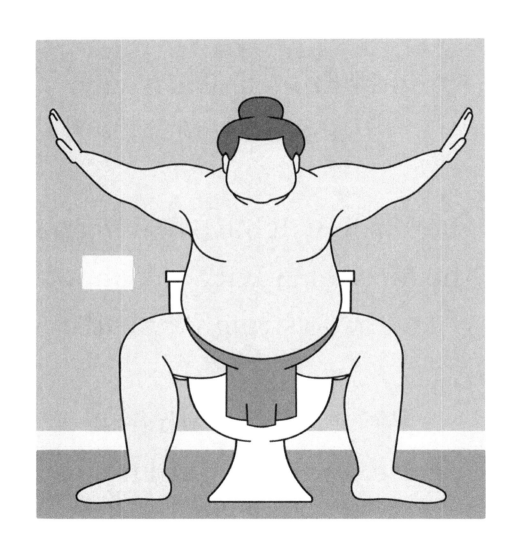

THE SUMO SHITTER

Imagine being a gigantic sumo wrestler, one of those who could easily break the toilet...

good, now do the wrestlers' ritual, beat the balls on the ground, spread your arms and sit down powerfully.

Push until your opponent comes out of the hole!

THE BROWN FLAMINGO

The flamingo move is a mix between relaxing and meditative...

repeat the position as shown, but be careful not to shit on your calf!

To avoid this, lean back slightly.

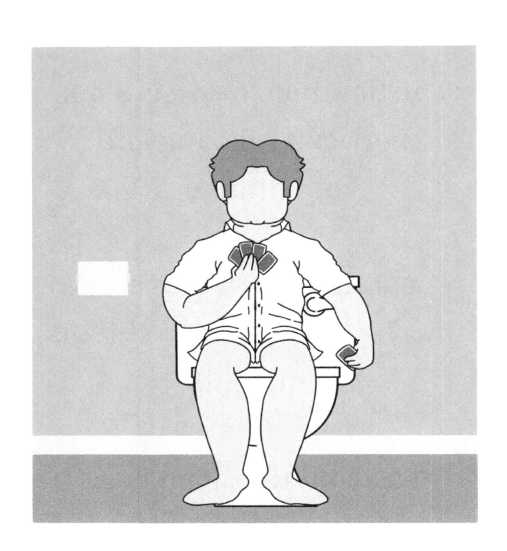

THE GAME LEAVES ME IN UNDERWEAR

There are those who stay in their underwear playing and there are those who play in the bathroom...

we suggest puzzles and solitaire games, the smartphone is already too attached to our hands, but for the more daring and less shy you can also play cards or other 1vs1 games.

THE LAUNCH OF THE ROCHET

One of the most satisfying positions ever consists of placing your knees on the board and leaning with your hands on the ground.

Take aim and lean enough to hit the hole, but if you don't make it on the first shot don't worry, it's an advanced technique and takes time!

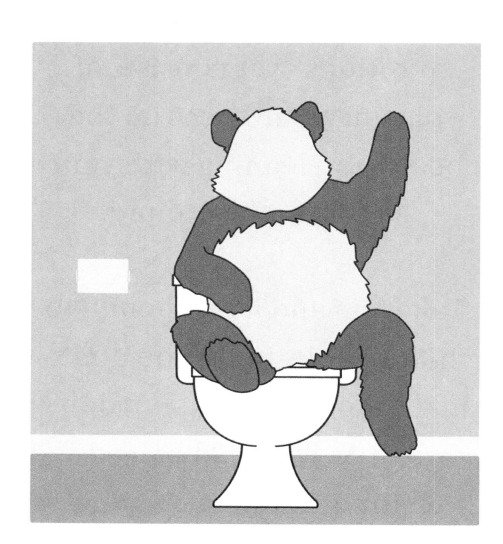

THE TAMED PANDA

Do you know what Pandas look like? Slow, clumsy, lazy and even a little stupid...

This position is inspired by their way of life... Sit on the toilet as if it were a sofa, or a eucalyptus plant, and shit as you want!
It doesn't matter if you don't hit the mark...

THE ASSHOLE COP

This position is for those who have never experienced the thrill of running a checkpoint...

Take the toilet brush and wave it every time you hear "ploff", alternatively do it every time you see someone pass by the window.

Please don't draw your weapon though!

THE POWER RANGER

Who has never seen power rangers and their extravagant moves...

With this move you can finally go back to being a child, copy the figure and add all the most ridiculous movements that come to mind.

It's definitely going to suck.

THE SACRED NINJA RITUAL

Did you know that ninjas are fast and silent like no other fighter in history?

Well with this pose you too will be able to shit silently and quickly.

We recommend placing some toilet paper on the bottom to avoid splashes!

THE SUPER SAYAN

ATTENTION:

If you push too hard you could burst a vein or break the toilet.

This is the Saiyan move, to implement it you have to shout very loudly, really loudly!

Do this until you see the tiles come off the floor, or until you finish shitting.

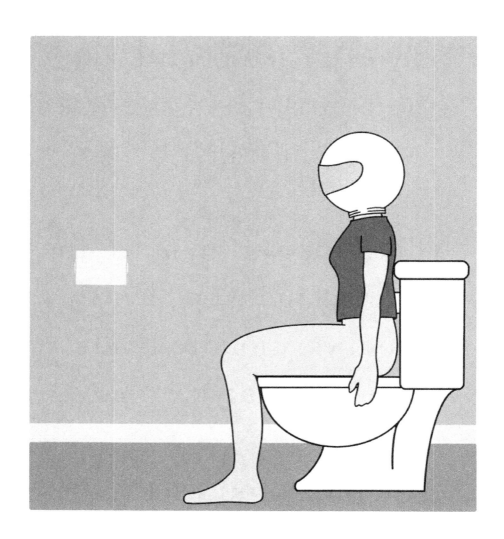

THE JOURNEY IN DEEP HOLE

Sometimes shitting is like a high-speed race...

To always remain safe, wear a helmet and fit well into the seat.

Move your right foot when you want to push hard and use the toilet brush as a handbrake when you arrive.

THE WATERING CAN

Technique not recommended
if you respect the place where
you defecate.

Get ready standing, legs open
and pants down.

Start watering everything you
see in front of you until you
start pooping.

Do this standing while
admiring the lake you created.

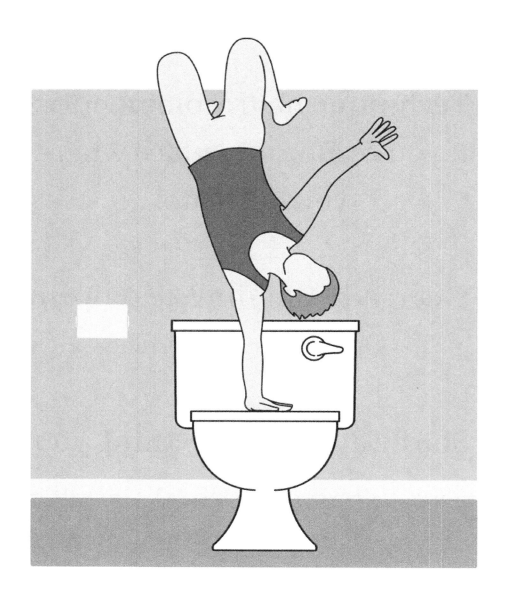

THE EXHIBITIONIST

Position truly for a few, only for acrobats or calisthenics practitioners.

He places his hand on the edge of the tablet, throws his feet up to the sky and bends a little.

Try to shit while you harden all the muscles to support yourself, the only satisfaction will be that of having succeeded.

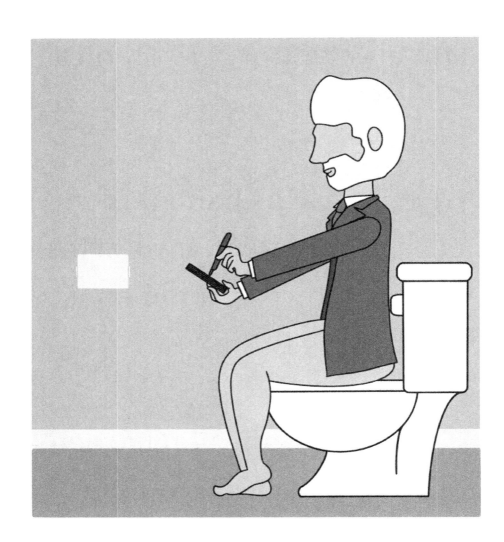

THE SPEECH GOES ON

Useful position for all teachers and students that are home schooled.

Take the device and sit on the toilet, shit calmly, but remember to disconnect the microphone and also the webcam if it's too harsh and you can see it on your face!

THE DECISIVE LUNGE

Have you skipped leg training recently? Or have you never even thought about it?

Why not combine business with pleasure and train a bit while you shit!

Go up and down in the position indicated in the image and change legs every 15 lunges!

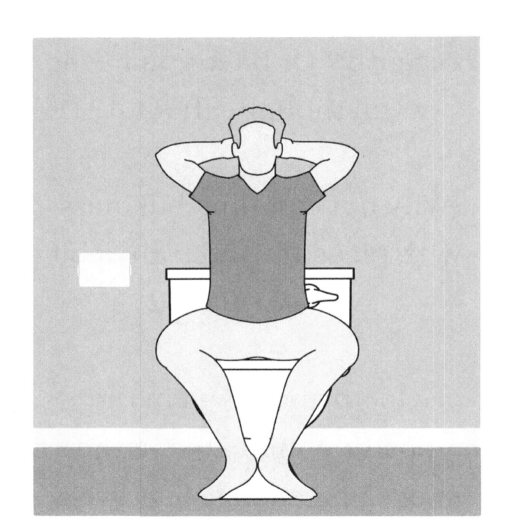

THE ART OF NOT DOING NOTHING

One thing is sure...

Even if you don't do anything you still get away!

However, if you do a lot, at least when you are on the crate, take a moment to relax, copy the position in the figure and enjoy a few minutes of liberation.

THE PROUD ARTIST

Just like a proud artist, who is not ashamed of anything, take a shit in your hand and throw it in the toilet with style.

But remember, a true artist never makes mistakes, so if you don't hit the mark it's better if you retire!

THE BOMB!

This very powerful technique can cause damage to the plumbing system, so be careful.

Replicate the position in the figure, count down for 10 seconds and then discharge everything you have at maximum power.

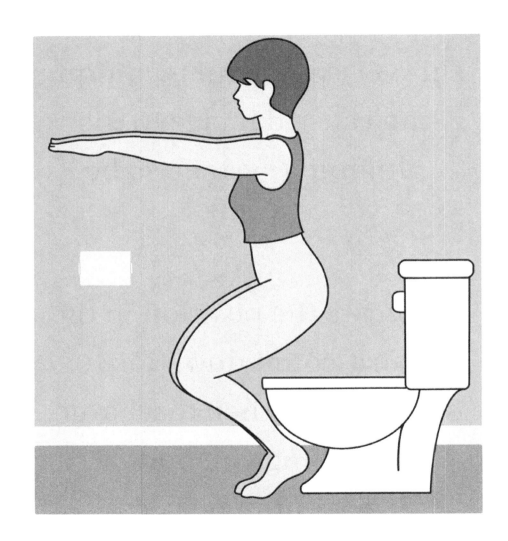

GYMNASTICS HELPS HERE IT IS HOW

Did you know that gymnastics helps you defecate better?

Why not do some to increase the stimulation!?

Replicate the figure and move up and down, but be prepared with your pants down because the need could be sudden!

THE POSSESSED

Position for lovers of the genre.

Replicate the worst possessions by placing your hands and feet on the ground, with your belly facing towards the other, and see if you can do it like this.

If you can't, don't worry, demons don't really need to poop.

FECAL MEDITATION

Purify your mind and relax, try to raise your self to a higher level...

With the right amount of training you will be able to meditate and shit at the same time, you will also be able to experiment with leavening, thus avoiding all the splashes!

WISDOM DOES SHIT

Replicate this position as a wise oriental meditator, whether you are more or less young, you will feel pervaded by a particular wisdom.

Try to treasure it, because as soon as you finish on the toilet, you will go back to being as before and all your powers will vanish.

CONSTIPATION AND GRACE

Both for constipated and non-constipated people, position to stretch the whole body in view of the great undertaking to be accomplished in a few moments.

Replicate the figure and bend in both directions, reversing the arm movements.

If you feel the urge, stop and proceed to evacuate.

SPIDER TOILET

Super hero position, upside down on the toilet.

Be careful not to make a mess like spider-pork.

Push slowly and lean slightly.

If you can't lower yourself from above, stick to a wall like a real spider.

LEGENDS
SUBWAYS
NEW YORKERS....

It is said that from time to time people in New York get sucked into the toilet by a fearsome sewer monster...

If you are in those areas, always be careful before sitting down, if necessary drop it on the ground and then pick it up.

THE ENTHUSIAST ASSHOLE

Have you ever tried toilet jumping?

Well you should, sometimes it doesn't take much to have fun!

Take a running start and jump with your legs apart... too simple?

Then try to shit in the meantime, obviously it's not worth it if you don't hit the hole!

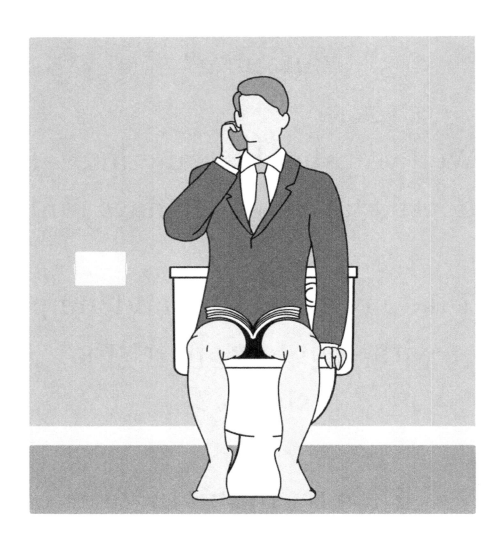

SMART WORKING IN ITALY

Who has never shit during a business meeting?

If you haven't done it, you can fix it now, call a customer or supplier while you're on the toilet and try not to get caught!

SOMETHING HAS GONE WRONG

Sometimes the discomfort comes from above and not from below...

in those cases we recommend the position shown in the figure, not only because it is comfortable, but also because it allows you to stretch in the meantime, which is something you know how to do very well for your body.

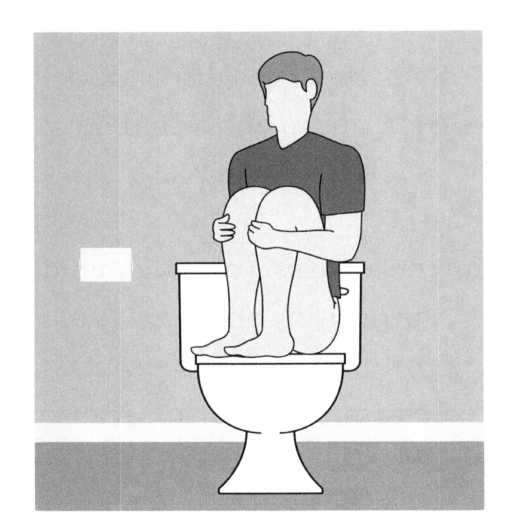

I SHIT MYSELF BECAUSE OF FEAR

There are times when you feel scared and other times when you are afraid of the shit you have to do...

in any case the correct position is the following, it helps to stimulate the session more and to end the nightmare as soon as possible!

DON'T SIT THERE ABOVE

This figure doesn't need much explanation...

Whether there's a monster in the toilet, or the toilet itself is monstrous, sometimes it's better not to shit at all.

EVERY PLACE IS FINE

The post-eaten shit is a classic, as is the drowsiness...

If you don't want to waste time, you can join things together, but always remember to keep one foot on the board, otherwise you could slip and hurt yourself.

I THOUGHT IT WAS ONE CARRIAGE, BUT....

Sometimes a nice royal toilet is much better than any luxurious carriage...

She shits like a princess, which in the end is a bit like everyone else does, only with more class!

For this position you need a crown, even a small or paper one is fine.

I THOUGHT IT WAS GOOD, INSTEAD IT'S SHIT

How many times have you found yourself in this situation?
You eat something a little extreme and after 10 minutes you have it liquid like never before...
This is also called Snow White's shit, but it has absolutely nothing white about it.

Clean the toilet thoroughly after you're done.

SOMETHING HAS GONE WRONG

The destroyer of worlds technique is one of the most satisfying, but never do it at home because it is very likely that you will be left without a toilet once the session is over.

The only rule in this situation is 'use all available force'.

TESTS OF MAGIC

If you like magic and illusion, or if you're just training for a show, the trick you need to try is the horizontal-suspended poop.

You will need the help of a magician to do this, find one you trust, when it comes to poop you can't improvise!

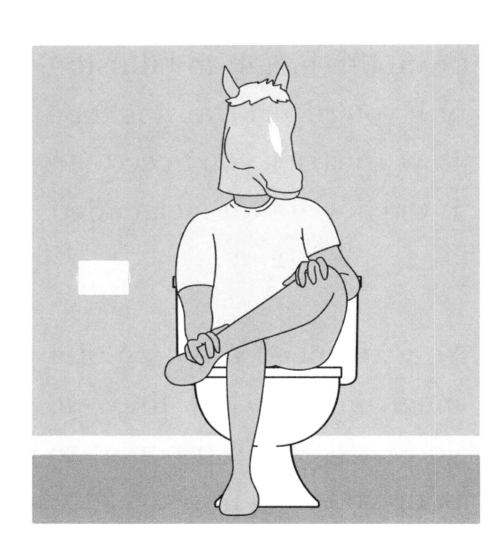

WE ARE RIDING A HORSE

Here there are 2 options:

get on all fours and shit like a horse
get a horse mask and shit as much as a horse

In both cases you will have completed the mission successfully.

BLIND SHOOTING

This position is the most exciting as the chances of success are not very high!

Replicate the figure trying to do the geometric and physical calculations well in order to center the hole.

If you can't make it, remember to clean up well, after all we are adventurers, not animals.

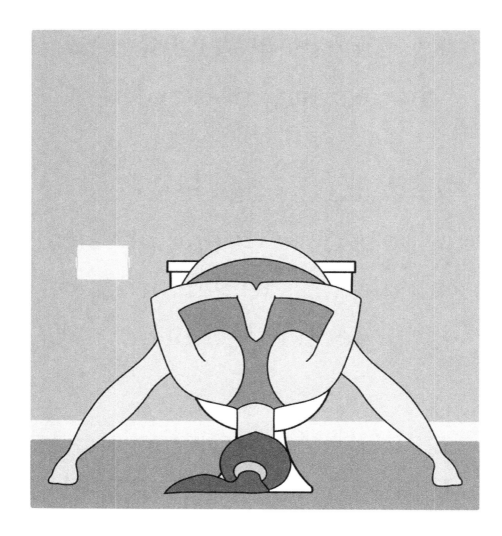

A DISTORTED VISION

Really impressive yoga pose, pooping like this will be really strange, but equally pleasant.

Make sure you have someone at home when you try this position for the first few times, you could be stuck like this for a long time!

Not recommended with the spring.

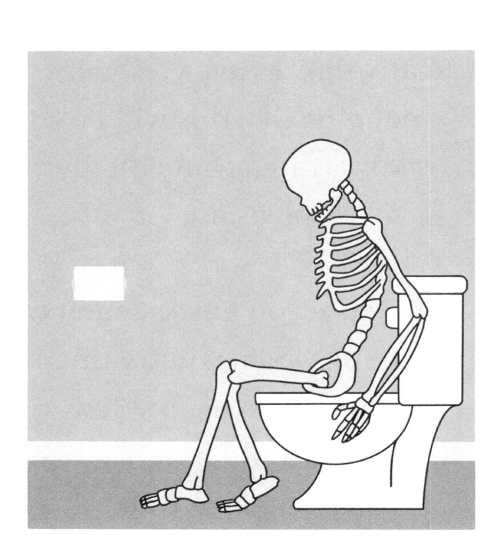

DON'T WORY, I WON'T GET MUCH TIME IN THE BATHROOM

Who hasn't become a skeleton waiting for him to come down?

In these cases there isn't much to do, exhale on the toilet or give up your seat to someone else...

The choice is yours.

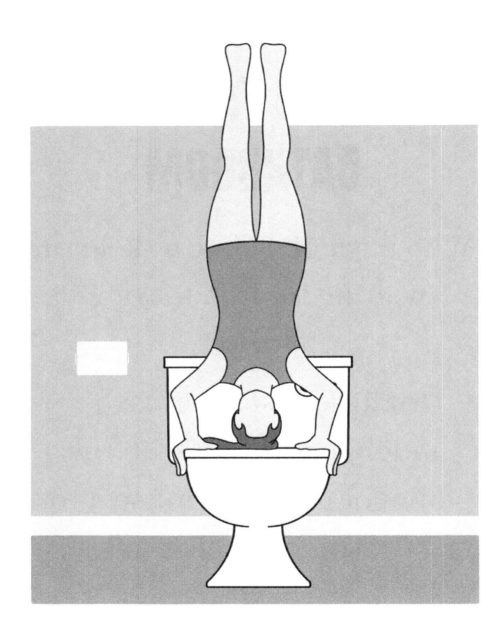

TRIP TO THE CENTER OF THE EARTH

This technique is very delicate, the slightest mistake would take you inside the earth's core and you would probably not come back alive.

Lower yourself as far as possible into the toilet and try to shit in it from the inside.

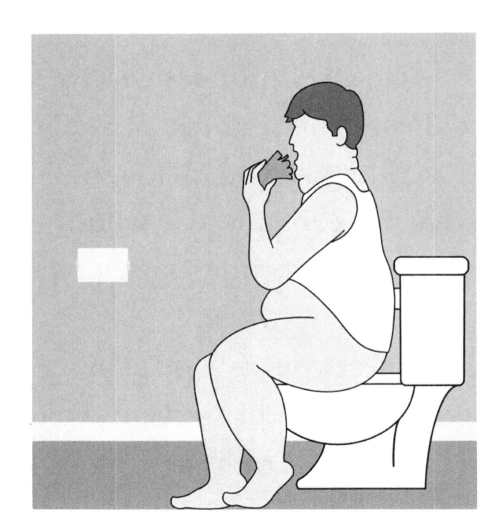

TO COMBINE THE PROFIT TO DELIGHTFUL

Why not have a nice local shit?

You'll discover that eating on the toilet is the most convenient thing ever, and it also saves time!

Even a nice coffee and a cigarette are great for shitting.

DANCING ON IT
THE WC

There are those who eat, those who smoke, those who act like Spider-Man and even those who dance on the toilet.

In this case we suggest a series of pirouettes that will make you dizzy and fall directly onto the board.

If you can handle it, try taking a shit while you dance.

THE BIG FOOT

Also called big foot, no one knows how these beings poop, also because despite the legends, no one has ever actually seen one.

What we can imagine is that you lose hair on the toilet seat, so if you are shaved you won't be able to replicate this move.

SHITTING ON THE TOWELS

You will love shitting hanging from the sheets, you can do it upside down, diagonally or split...

or maybe all 3!

With this technique you will be able to give free rein to your imagination and shit in a truly original way.

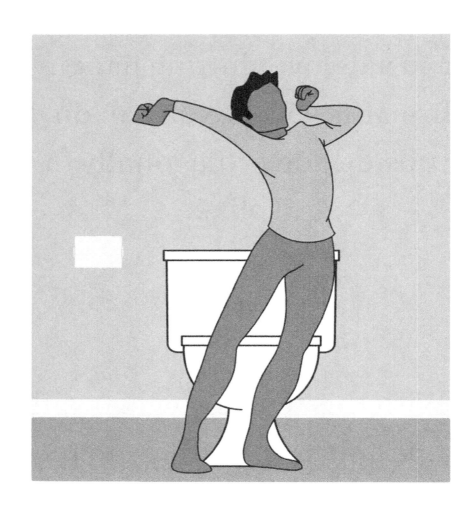

SHIT IN EXTENSION

Extended shitting is more common in the morning, when you are not yet fully awake and you stretch to wake up your nerves and muscles.

The distension of these will also cause the urge to awaken and you will be able to defecate with great pleasure.

THIS IS BETTER

It is said that a yoga guru, holding a lesson for his students, let out a very wet fart which inspired this caccoid position.

To be replicated only in the event of a spring or otherwise it will be ineffective.

THE CANDLE

One of the classics.

The candle remains one of the best positions for shitting without getting splashed, it is also valid by placing your feet somewhere, as long as the figure always respects the appearance of a candle.

DEDICATION

The scene is a bit like Peter Griffin forgetting how to sit, only here the act is driven by a total dedication to shitting.

Throw yourself towards the toilet with passion, if it's true love it will be fine.

EXTREME DEFENSE

Unfortunately sometimes our throne is threatened by external agents, take a sword, a stick or a toilet brush and prepare to defend it!

In the meantime, open a hole on the back of your trousers and shit at your leisure, after all, you're there on purpose!

Balance

Raising your legs always works to give that extra fluidity to the poop, but doing it on one leg is a style exercise that not only works, but also helps to increase balance over time.

Warmly recommended to everyone!

KUNG FU POOP

For the most aggressive, here is the kung fu poop position, which basically consists of throwing powerful kicks at imaginary enemies and shitting at the same time.

Only true kung fu warriors will pass the test.

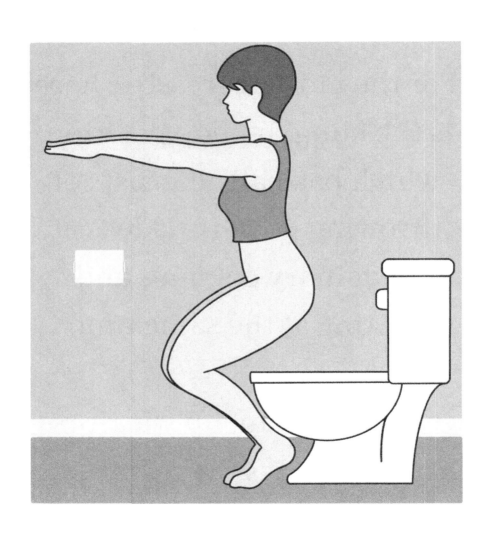

GYMNASTICS HELPS HERE IT IS HOW!

As already seen in other positions, physical exercise always helps expulsion.

A few squats with hands forward are ideal to increase the stimulus.

If it doesn't work it's because you're not doing enough...
If it really doesn't work, at least you will have strengthened your legs!

MESY CAT

Cats are known for putting themselves in strange places, the problem comes when they put themselves right on the toilet!

The following technique involves shitting while avoiding the cat or farting so loudly that it runs away.

THE BORED

There are also those who get bored and spend their time on the toilet...

However, sitting all the time is tiring, so you can wander around the bathroom with your trousers down and whenever you feel like doing it wherever you want.

If he's outside at least you found something to do... like clean.

THE FATAL DISCOLORATION

Some poop can hurt or even
be lethal... To avoid the worst,
vent against the wall or a
cabinet and then lie down to
let your vent hole rest!

THE HERO OF SHIT

If you have fallen into a container of shit you have developed the incredible power of shitting out your hands, at that point free rein to your crap.

Millions of people will envy you, but remember...

Great responsibilities come from great powers.

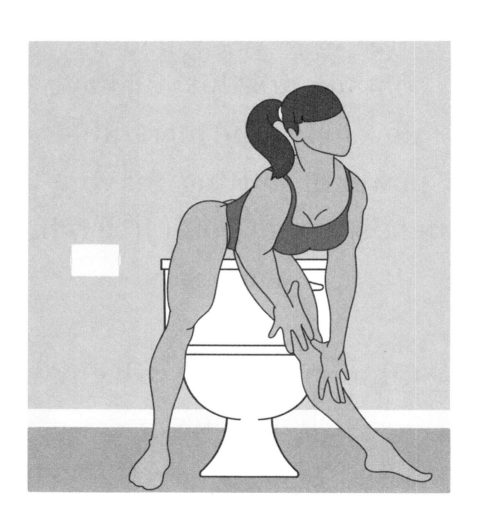

THE EXHIBITIONIST

Who says bathroom selfies are only taken in the mirror?

Why not do them while you're pooping and show off your body a nit?

It would be a great excuse.

The most important thing is flexing!

PARKOUR

The heart oil or Michael Scott move is one of the coolest ever!

Put your hand somewhere and make a ridiculous jump and totally unnecessary, of course also remember to shit in the meantime!

Everything is fine as long as it is cringe.

REVERSO

Especially nice if above the toilet there is a window...

Sit on the toilet backwards, like it's a bidet, and enjoy the shit.

Pay attention to not put your thing down, if you have it, who knows what diseases you might catch!

DIVINE SIGN

You know too, sometimes it takes the help of the Most High to get it down...

Invoke your divinity and raise your hands to heaven, sooner or later a signal will come...

If nothing happens you have invoked the wrong God, try another one!

THANKS!

We hope you enjoyed reading this book, if you liked it and even if you received it as a gift you might leave a positive feedback on Amazon and share it with your friends! On TikTok can be very successful as well, make a video while you browse it!

Printed in Great Britain
by Amazon